M000195990

Principia Astrologia de Financial

Course 1

2017

M. G. BUCHOLTZ, B.Sc., MBA

Wood Dragon Books

Box 1216, Regina, Saskatchewan, Canada, S4P 3B4

www.wooddragonbooks.com

ISBN# 978-0-9953342-3-6

Copyright 2017 Malcolm Bucholtz, B.Sc., MBA

Printed in Canada

All rights reserved. This book or any portion thereof may not be reproduced or used in any manner whatsoever without the express written permission of the author except for the use of brief quotations in a critical review.

Contents

Figures and Quizes

Acknowledgements

To the many traders and investors who at a visceral level
suspect there is more to the financial market complex than
P/E ratios and analyst recommendations. You are correct.
There is more. Your open mind tells you there is much more.
The markets are in fact rooted in astronomical and
astrological timing. This learning course will add a whole new
dimension to your market activities.

Disclaimer

All material provided herein is based on material gleaned from mathematical and astrological publications researched by the author to supplement his own trading. This publication is written with sincere intent for those who actively trade and invest in the financial markets and who are looking to incorporate astrological phenomena and esoteric math into their market activity. While the material presented herein has proven reliable to the author in his personal trading and investing activity, there is no guarantee the material herein will continue to be reliable into the future. The author and publisher assume no liability whatsoever for any investment or trading decisions made by readers of this book. The reader alone is responsible for all trading and investment outcomes and is further advised not to exceed his or her risk tolerances when trading or investing on the financial markets.

Recommended Readings

The Bull, the Bear and the Planets, M.G. Bucholtz, (iUniverse, USA, 2013)

The Lost Science, M.G. Bucholtz, (iUniverse, USA, 2013)

The Cosmic Clock, M.G. Bucholtz (Wood Dragon Books, Canada, 2016)

The Universal Clock, J. Long, (P.A.S. Publishing, USA,)

McWhirter Theory of Stock Market Forecasting, L. McWhirter, (Astro Book Company, USA, 1938)

The Universe Within, N. Turok, (House of Anansi Press, Canada, 2012)

A Theory of Continuous Planet Interaction, Tony Waterfall, *NCGR Research Journal, Volume 4, Spring 2014*, pp67-87.

Introduction

Many market analysts and financial media commentators think daily news, quarterly earnings reports and corporate events drive stock prices.

I disagree.

There is something else that drives the financial markets. I have two opinions on what this something else might be.

The first opinion is that the financial markets are a reflection of the mass psychological emotion of traders, investors and fund managers. The term *reflection* may even be too mild of a descriptor. It may be more accurate to boldly state that human emotion drives buying and selling decisions in the financial markets. When market participants are feeling positive, they are driven to buy. When they are feeling uncertain or negative, they are driven to sell.

Probing this idea deeper immediately yields the complex question - what drives human emotion?

Medical researchers still have not definitively answered this question. Some say changes in blood alkalinity or acidity impact our emotions. Some say changes in chemical hormones in the bloodstream are the cause. My humble opinion on this complex matter is that the ever-changing configurations of orbiting planets and other celestial bodies in our cosmos influence our body chemistry and thereby drive human emotion.

This opinion has been shaped by the many Astrology publications I have read over the past several years including Tony Waterfall's insightful article from the *Spring 2014 NCGR Research Journal.* In his article Waterfall reminds readers that the Sun is the centre of our planetary system. The Sun emits massive amounts of solar radiation in all directions into the vastness of space. This radiation is called *solar wind.* This solar wind interacts with the magnetic fields around Mercury,

Venus, Moon, Mars, Jupiter, Saturn, Uranus, Neptune and Pluto. These planets accept and then disburse the solar wind radiation. As the radiation is disbursed, a goodly amount of it finds its way towards the magnetic field around planet Earth. Changes in the density and speed of solar wind mean that the amount of radiation reaching Earth's magnetic field on a daily, weekly or monthly basis will be ever-changing. As a result, the intensity or flux of the Earth's magnetic field is also constantly changing. The alignment of the orbiting planets at any given time in our cosmos plays a key role in determining how much solar radiation is deflected towards Earth's magnetic field. A simplistic way of viewing this entire arrangement is to think of a billiards table as the cosmos. The various balls on the table are the planets and other celestial bodies. The solar radiation is the white cue ball bouncing and deflecting off other balls on the table. The human body is largely comprised of water. We all have an electrical field that runs through our tissues. Hence, basic physics demands that changes to the Earth's magnetic field will then induce subtle changes to our bodily electric circuitry. These subtle changes, in my opinion, are what drive our emotional responses. But there is so much more to be understood. Scientists and psychologists who are on a quest to learn more have come to call the developing science of how the cosmos affects humans *cosmo-biology*.

Ancient civilizations as far back as the Babylonians too recognized cosmo-biology, but in a more rudimentary form. Their high priests tracked and recorded changes in the emotions of the people. These diviners and seers also tracked events, both fortuitous and disastrous. Although they lacked the ability to comprehend the physics of solar wind and magnetic fields, they were able to visually spot the planets Mercury, Venus, Mars, Jupiter and Saturn in the heavens. They correlated changes in human emotion and changes in societal events to these planets. They assigned to these planets the names of the various Deities revered by the people. They further identified and named various star constellations in the heavens and further divided the heavens into twelve signs. This was the birth of Astrology as we know it today.

Starting in the early 1900's, esoteric thinkers such as the famous Wall Street trader W.D. Gann noted that basic Astrology bore a striking correlation to changes on the financial markets. This was the birth of Financial Astrology. Gann based his writings and forecasts on the synodic cycles between various planets. Gann also delved deep into esoteric math, notably square root math. He is well remembered for Gann Lines – a technique based on square roots. But Gann lived in a challenging time. Statute laws in places like New York expressly forbade the use of occult science in business ventures. Gann therefore carefully concealed the basis for his market forecasts. Today many traders and investors try to emulate Gann but they do so in a linear fashion – looking for repetitive cycles on the calendar. What they are missing is the Astrology component, which is anything but linear.

In the 1930s, Louise McWhirter followed closely in Gann's footsteps. She identified an 18.6 year cyclical correlation between the general state of the American economy and the position of the North Node of Moon. Her methodology also extended to include the Moon passing by key points of the 1792 natal birth horoscope of the New York Stock Exchange. As well, she identified a correlation between price movement of a stock and those times when transiting Sun, Mars, Jupiter and Saturn made hard aspects to the natal Sun position in the stock's natal birth horoscope.

The late 1940s saw even further advancements in the field of Financial Astrology when astrologer Garth Allen (a.k.a. Donald Bradley) produced his Siderograph Model. This complex model is based on aspects between the various transiting planets. Each aspect as it occurs is given a sinusoidal weighting as the *orb* between the planets varies. This model is as powerful today as it was in the late 1940s.

Have you been to a casino lately? Did you win or lose? Regardless of your outcome, that casino did not run by itself. Somewhere behind the scenes is the operator of the show. The slot machines are all carefully programmed to give odds in favor of the casino. The number of decks that the blackjack dealer uses has been determined so as to place the odds in favor of the casino. My second opinion on what drives financial markets is a brazen one and it follows this casino analogy. This opinion bluntly says that the markets are manipulated from deep within New York, London and other financial centers. This manipulation is based around astrological cycles and occurrences. This manipulation carefully places the odds in favor of those doing the manipulating. It is even quite possible that once efforts to "move" the markets are underway at these various astrological points in time, human emotion kicks in and media frenzy takes over. As you read these words, I invite you to think back to August 2015 and the market selloff that apparently nobody saw coming. The reality is that this selloff started during a Venus Retrograde event and the subsequent appearance of Venus as a Morning star after having been only visible as an Evening star for the past 263 days. What about the early days of 2016 when Mercury was Retrograde and the markets hit a rough patch? What about the weakness of June 2016 when Venus emerged from Conjunction to become visible as an Evening Star? What about the 2016 US Presidential Election where markets were slumping for weeks in advance. Then suddenly – when the average person was throwing in the towel out of sheer pessimism – the markets did an about-face and started to rally higher. The placement of the planets at the New Moon event prior to Election day suggested a coming trend change as did Venus being at its declination minimum. If these various market events were subtle manipulation, think about how much short term trading profit was made by the insiders.

I personally began to embrace Financial Astrology in 2012 which was a monumental shift given that my educational background comprises an Engineering degree and an MBA degree. Two linear-thinking, left-brain degrees to be sure. Since 2012, my research and back-testing has satisfied me that a correlation does indeed exist between Astrology and the financial markets.

This 3-part series of learning Courses which I have titled *Principia Astrologia de Financial* is designed to offer you the principles of Financial Astrology which you can then apply to your trading and investing.

Course 1, begins by offering insight into the language and images of Astrology. What then follows is an examination of concepts such as Declination, Elongation, Retrograde and Conjunctions. Along the way, you will be challenged to quizzes to ensure that your learning is on track. I have included many examples to show you how these various concepts have influenced stocks, indices and commodities. As you work your way through this Course, you can easily start to apply your new-found knowledge to your market activity.

When applying Astrology to trading and investing, it is vital at all times to be aware of the price trend. There are many ways of observing trend. My personal experience has shown me that the chart indicators developed by J. Welles Wilder are very effective at identifying trend changes. In particular, the Directional Movement Indicator (DMI) and the Volatility Stop are two indicators that should be taken seriously. As a trader and investor, what you are looking for is a change of trend that aligns to an astrological event. When you see the trend change, you should take action. Whether that action is implementing a long position, a short position or just tightening up on a stop loss will depend on your personal appetite for risk and on your investment and trading objectives. Astrology is not about trying to take action at each and every astrological event that comes along. Not all events are powerful enough to induce a change of trend. Hence, that is why I advise to be alert at each astrological event and to keep your eye open for changes in trend.

I sincerely hope after you have applied the material in Course 1 to your trading and investing activity, you will start to embrace Financial Astrology as a valuable tool.

1. Astrology Fundamentals

Astrology is an ancient science focused on the correlation between the planets, events of nature and behaviour of mankind. This ancient science is rooted in thousands of years of observation across many civilizations.

- The ancient Sumerians, Akkadians and Babylonians between the 4th and 2nd centuries BC believed the affairs of mankind could be gauged by watching the motions of certain stars and planets. They recorded their predictions and future indications of prosperity and calamity on clay tablets. These early recordings form the foundation of modern day Astrology.

- Ancient Egyptian artifacts show that high priests Petosiris and Necepso who lived during the reign of Ramses II were revered for their knowledge of Astrology. The Egyptian culture is thought to have developed a 12 month x 30 day time keeping method based on the repeated appearances of constellations.

- Ancient Indian and Chinese artifacts reveal that Astrology held an esteemed place in those societies for many thousands of years.

- Hipparchus, Pythagoras and Plato are key names from the Greek era. Historians think Pythagoras assigned mathematical values to the relations between celestial bodies. Plato is thought to have offered up predictions relating celestial bodies to human fates. Hipparchus is thought to have compiled a star catalogue which popularized Astrology.

- In the latter years of the Roman empire, Astrology was used for political gain. Important military figures surrounded themselves with philosophers such as Ptolemy and Valens. In 126 AD, Ptolemy penned four books describing the influence of the stars. His works are collectively called the *Tetrabiblos*. In 160 AD, Valens penned *Anthologies* in which he further summarized the principles of Astrology.

Following the conversion of Emperor Constantine to Christianity in 312 AD, using Astrology for gain became a crime according to the Church of Rome. Astrology then began a slow retreat to the sidelines where for the most part it remains today. Despite Astrology having been sidelined by a Church seeking to protect its authority, Astrology was still used by leading thinkers such as Galileo, Brahe, Nostradamus, Kepler, Bacon and Newton. Thanks to the tenacity of these men, Astrology was prevented from fading away altogether into a distant memory.

The Zodiac

The Sun is at the center of our solar system. The Earth, Moon, planets and various other asteroid bodies complete our planetary system. The various planets and other asteroid bodies rotate 360 degrees around the Sun following a path called the ecliptic plane as shown in Figure 1. Earth is slightly tilted (approximately 23 degrees) relative to the ecliptic plane. Projecting the Earth's equator into space produces the celestial equator plane. By mathematical definition, two planes that are not parallel must intersect. There are two points of intersection between the ecliptic plane and celestial equator plane. These points are commonly called the vernal equinox (occurring at March 20th) and the autumnal equinox (occurring at September 20th). Dividing the ecliptic plane into twelve equal sections of 30 degrees results in what astrologers call the Zodiac. The twelve portions of the Zodiac have names including Aries, Cancer, Leo and so on. If these names sound familiar, they should. You routinely see all twelve names in the daily horoscope section of your morning newspaper. Figure 2 illustrates a Zodiac wheel. The starting point or zero degree point of the zodiac wheel is the sign Aries, located at the vernal equinox of each year.

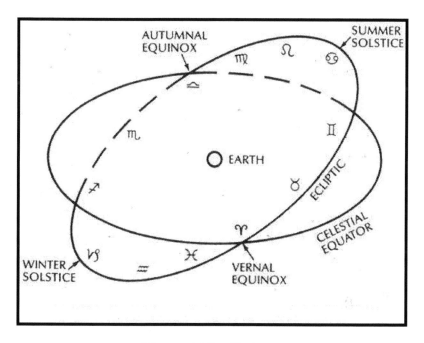

Figure 1 The Ecliptic

Figure 2 The Zodiac Wheel

If you have ever wondered about the names of the Zodiac wheel portions, the following descriptions may be of interest. To ancient civilizations, each of these twelve signs was named after groupings and patterns of stars visible in the heavens to the high priests.

Aries (The Ram)

(0 to 30 degrees) 21 March – 20 April

According to Greek mythology, Nephele, the mother of Phrixus and Helle, gave her sons a ram with a golden fleece. To escape their evil stepmother, Hera, the sons mounted the ram and fled. When they reached the sea, Helles fell into the water and perished. Phrixus survived the ordeal and upon arriving in Colchis was received by King Aeetes who sacrificed the ram and dedicated the fleece to Zeus. Zeus then transported the ram into the heavens and made it into a constellation.

Taurus (The Bull)

(30 to 60 degrees) 21 April – 21 May

According to Roman legend, Jupiter took the form of a bull and became infatuated with the fair maiden Europa. When Europa decided to ride the bull, it rushed into the sea and whisked Europa off to Crete. Jupiter then raised the bull into the heavens where it became a star.

Gemini (The Twins)

(60 to 90 degrees) 22 May – 21 June

In Greek mythology, Hercules and Apollo are twins. In Roman legend, these twins are said to be Castor and Pollux, the sons of Leda. Pollux was the son of Zeus, who seduced Leda, while Castor was the son of Tyndareus, King of Sparta. Castor and Pollux are mythologically associated with St. Elmo's fire in their role as protectors of sailors. When Castor died, because he was mortal, Pollux begged Zeus to give Castor immortality. Zeus granted the wish by uniting Castor and Pollux together in the heavens as a constellation.

Cancer (The Crab)

(90 to 120 degrees) 22 June-23 July

Roman legend says that Cancer is the crab that bit Hercules during his fight with the Hydra monster. The crab was then placed in the heavens as a star by Juno, the enemy of Hercules.

Leo (The Lion)

(120 to 150 degrees) 24 July – 23 August

Legend says that Hercules battled with the Nemean lion and won. Zeus raised the lion to the heavens as a star.

Virgo (The Virgin)

(150 to 180 degrees) 24 August – 23 September

Legend has it that Virgo is a constellation modelled after Justitia, daughter of Astraeus and Ancora. Justitia lived before mankind sinned. After mankind sinned, Justitia returned to the heavens.

Libra (The Scales)

(180 to 210 degrees) 24 September – 23 October

Libra was known in Babylonian astronomy as a set of scales that were held sacred to the Sun God Shamash, the patron of truth and justice. In Roman mythology, Libra is considered to depict the scales held by Astraea , the Goddess of Justice.

Scorpio (The Scorpion)

(210 to 240 degrees) 24 October – 22 November

According to Greek mythology, Orion boasted to Diana and Latona that he could kill every animal on Earth. The ladies sent for a scorpion which stung Orion to death. Jupiter then raised the scorpion to the heavens as a constellation.

Sagittarius (The Archer)

(240 to 270 degrees) 23 November – 22 December

In Babylonian legend, Sagittarius was the God of War. In Greek legend, Sagittarius was a centaur (half man, half horse) in the act of shooting an arrow. In Roman legend, Sagittarius was a centaur who killed himself when he accidently dropped one of Hercules' poisoned arrows on his hoof.

Capricorn (The Goat)

(270 to 300 degrees) 23 December – 20 January

In Greek legend, during the war with the giants the Greek Gods were driven into Egypt. In order to escape the wrath of the encroaching giants, each Greek God changed his shape. The God Pan leapt into the river Nile and turned the upper part of his body into a goat and the lower part into a fish. This combination was deemed worthy by Jupiter who raised Pan to the heavens.

Aquarius (The Water Bearer)

(300 to 330 degrees) 21 January – 19 February

According to legend, Deucalion- the son of Prometheus, was raised to the heavens after surviving the great deluge that flooded the world.

Pisces (The Fishes)

(330 to 360 degrees) 20 February - 20 March

In Greek legend, Aphrodite and Eros were surprised by Typhon while playing along the river Nile. To escape, they jumped into the water and were changed into two fishes.

2. Basic Financial Astrology

The Celestial Bodies

In addition to the Sun and Moon, the eight celestial bodies Mercury, Venus, Mars, Jupiter, Saturn, Uranus, Neptune and Pluto are critical to Financial Astrology. Figure 3 illustrates these various bodies in orbit around the Sun on the ecliptic plane. The closest planet to the Sun is Mercury and it orbits the Sun in 88 days. Next closest is Venus with a 225 day orbital period. Next closest to the Sun is Earth with its 365 day period. The remaining bodies are all further afield and take longer to make their orbits. Jupiter for example takes 11.9 years and Saturn 29.5 years.

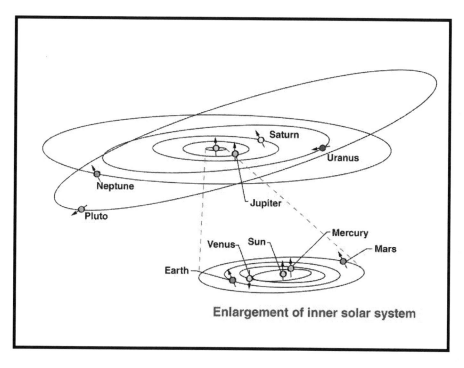

Figure 3 – The Planets

The Glyphs

These planets and the twelve signs of the Zodiac are denoted by strange looking symbols, called glyphs. Figure 4 presents the glyphs.

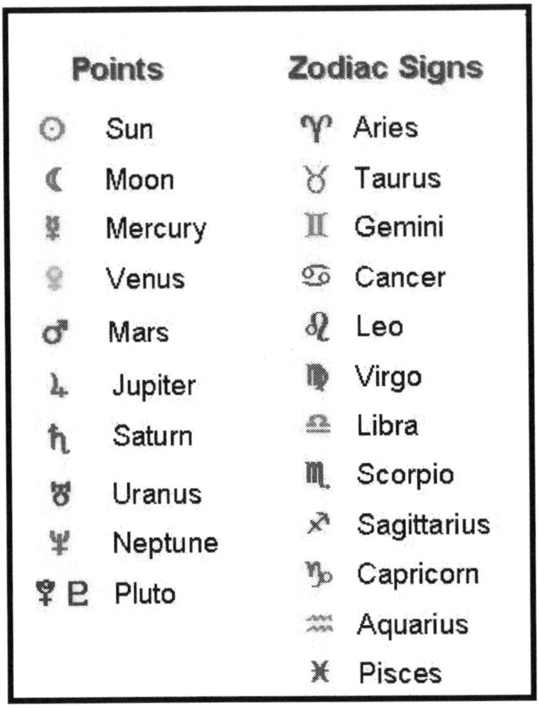

Points		Zodiac Signs	
☉	Sun	♈	Aries
☾	Moon	♉	Taurus
☿	Mercury	♊	Gemini
♀	Venus	♋	Cancer
♂	Mars	♌	Leo
♃	Jupiter	♍	Virgo
♄	Saturn	♎	Libra
♅	Uranus	♏	Scorpio
♆	Neptune	♐	Sagittarius
♇ ♇	Pluto	♑	Capricorn
		♒	Aquarius
		♓	Pisces

Figure 4 – The Glyphs

Ascendant, Descendant, MC and IC

As the Earth rotates on its axis once in every 24 hours, an observer situated on Earth will detect an apparent motion of the Zodiac. To better define this motion, astrologers apply four cardinal points to the Zodiac, almost like the north, south, east and west points on a compass. These cardinal points divide the Zodiac into four quadrants. The east point is termed the Ascendant and is often abbreviated Asc. The west point is termed the Descendant and is often abbreviated Dsc. The south point is termed the Mid-Heaven (from the Latin Medium

Coeli) and is often abbreviated MC. The north point is termed the Imum Coeli (Latin for bottom of the sky) and is abbreviated IC.

These cardinal points , as illustrated in Figure 5, will come into fashion in the second Course of this learning series when you will learn about the work of Louise McWhirter – a mysterious figure form the 1930s. Note also in Figure 5 that the Zodiac is broken into twelve numbered sections. These are called Houses and are vital to the more detailed models you will learn about in Course 2.

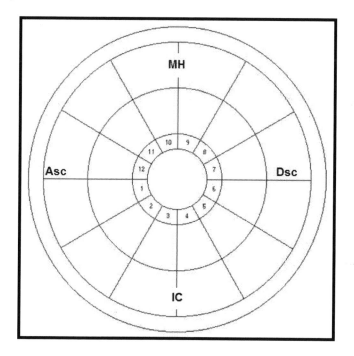

Figure 5 The Cardinal Points

Geocentric and Heliocentric Astrology

Financial Astrology comes in two distinct varieties – geocentric and heliocentric.

In geocentric Astrology, the Earth is the vantage point for observing the planets as they pass through the signs of the Zodiac. Owing to the

27

different times for the planets to each orbit the Sun, an astrologer situated on Earth would see the planets making distinct angles (called aspects) with one another and also with the Sun. The aspects that are commonly used in Astrology are 0, 30, 45, 60, 90, 120, 150 and 180 degrees. In Financial Astrology, it is common to refer to only the 0, 45, 90, 120 and 180 degree aspects.

In heliocentric Astrology, the Sun is the vantage point for observing the planets as they pass through the signs of the Zodiac. An observer positioned on the Sun would also see the orbiting planets making aspects with one another.

Aspects, especially the geocentric ones, are at the heart of the McWhirter model and also the Albano model which you will learn about.

The Moon

Just as the planets orbit 360 degrees around the Sun, the Moon orbits 360 degrees around the Earth. The Moon orbits the Earth in a plane of motion called the lunar orbit plane. This plane is inclined at about 5 degrees to the ecliptic plane as Figure 6 shows. The Moon orbits Earth with a slightly elliptical pattern in approximately 27.3 days, relative to an observer located on a fixed frame of reference such as the Sun. This time period is known as a *sidereal month*. However, during one sidereal month, an observer located on Earth (a moving frame of reference) will revolve part way around the Sun. To that Earth-bound observer, a complete orbit of the Moon around the Earth will appear longer than the sidereal month at approximately 29.5 days. This 29.5 day period of time is known as a *synodic month* or more commonly a lunar month. The lunar month plays a key role in applying Astrology to the financial markets. Some societies and religions, such as the Hebrew people, to this day still base their calendars around the concept of the lunar month.

The Moon figures prominently in the history and lore of Astrology. Throughout the centuries, the Moon has been associated with health, mood and dreams. In 6th century Constantinople (modern day Istanbul, Turkey), physicians at the court of Emperor Justinian advised that gout could be cured by inscribing verses of Homer on a copper plate when the Moon was in the sign of Libra or Leo. In 17th century France, astrologers used the Moon to explain mood changes in women. In 17th century England, herbal remedy practitioners advised people to pluck the petals of the peony flower when the Moon was waning. During the Renaissance period, it was thought that dreams could come true if the Moon was in the signs of Taurus, Leo, Aquarius or Scorpio.

Today, such ideas about the Moon are no more. But, the Moon nonetheless continues to be recognized as a powerful celestial body. Just as the gravitational pull of the Moon can influence the action of ocean tides, this same pull somehow also influences our emotions of fear and hope. As our emotions of fear and hope change, our investment buying and selling decisions also change. These emotional changes correlate to changes in price trend action. When this correlation is overlaid with technical chart analysis, a whole new dimension in trading and investing can open up to you.

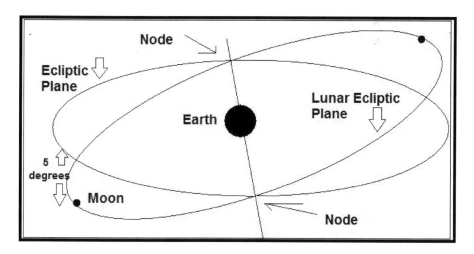

Figure 6 – The Nodes

The Nodes

Another mathematical construct central to Financial Astrology is the Nodes. The Nodes are the points of intersection between the ecliptic plane and the Moon's ecliptic plane. Figure 6 illustrates the Nodes. In Financial Astrology, typically only the North Node is referred to.

Retrograde

Think of the planets orbiting the Sun as a group of race cars travelling around a racetrack. Consider what happens as a fast moving car approaches a slower moving car from behind. At first, all appears normal. An observer in the fast moving car sees the slower moving car heading in the same direction. Gradually, the observer in the fast car sees that he will soon overtake the slow car. For a brief moment in time as the fast car overtakes the slower car the observer in the fast car notices that the slower car appears to stand still. Of course the slow car is not really standing still. This is simply an optical illusion.

These brief illusory periods are what astrologers call Retrograde events. To ancient societies, Retrograde events were of great significance as human emotion was often seen to be changeable at these events. To adherents of Financial Astrology, Mercury, Venus and Mars Retrograde events are vitally important times.

There will be three or four times during a year when Earth and Mercury pass by each other on this celestial racetrack. There will be one or perhaps two times per year when Earth and Venus pass each other. There will be one time every two years when Earth and Mars pass each other.

The diagram in Figure 7 illustrates the concept of Retrograde using Earth and Mercury.

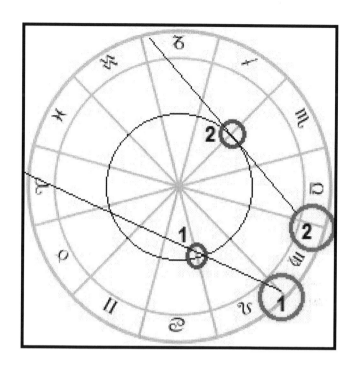

Figure 7 – The Retrograde Concept

In 30 days of time planet Earth (shown as the larger circles in the diagram) will travel 30 degrees of the zodiac (from point 1 to point 2). But, Mercury is a faster mover. In the same 30 days of time, Mercury (shown as the smaller circles) will travel through about 120 degrees of the zodiac (point 1 to point 2) – passing by Earth in the process. From our vantage point here on Earth, initially as Mercury is setting up to pass Earth, we see Mercury in the sign of Aries. As Mercury completes its trip past Earth, we see it in the sign of Capricorn. In other words, the way we see it here on Earth, Mercury has moved backwards as it passed Earth. This is the concept of Retrograde. To the ancients who did not fully understand how the cosmos worked, it must have been awe-inspiring to see a planet move backwards in the heavens relative to the constellation stars.

Declination

Declination refers to the positioning of a celestial body above or below the Earth's celestial equator plane. Recall, the equator plane is generated by taking the equator and extending it in all directions. Celestial bodies experience declinations of up to about 25 degrees above and below the celestial equator plane as viewed from our vantage point here on Earth.

My market back-testing research has revealed that changes in the declination of a celestial body can affect the financial markets.

Moon, Mercury, Venus, Mars and indeed Earth itself endure frequent changes in declination due to the gravitational force of the Sun. Planets like Jupiter, Saturn, Neptune, Uranus and Pluto also experience declination changes but these changes are slow to evolve because these planets are farther distant from the Sun and less affected by its gravitational pull. Scientists using mathematical models are able to generate declination plots for the various planets. Figure 8 illustrates the declination of Venus during 2017. Note that it will encounter a declination high in early March and then its maximum for the year will occur in August.

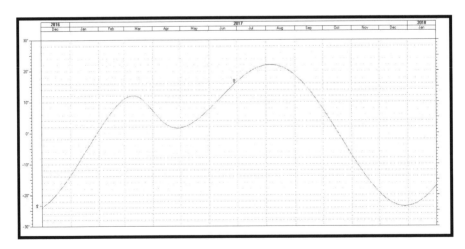

Figure 8 – The Declination Concept

Elongation and Separation

The orbit of a planet around the Sun is not a perfectly circular event. Rather, planets orbit the Sun in slightly elliptical paths.

From an observer's vantage point on Earth, there will be times when orbiting planets are seen to be at maximum angles of separation from the Sun. These events are what astronomers refer to as maximum easterly and westerly Elongations. In Financial Astrology, the Elongation of Mercury is a key concept. Figure 9 illustrates the Elongation concept using Mercury as an example.

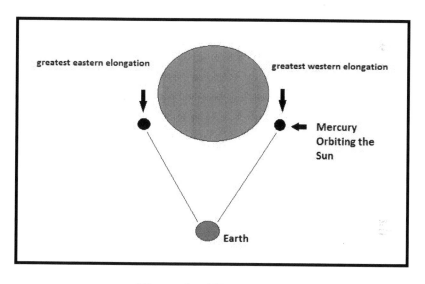

Figure 9 – The Elongation Concept

Conjunctions

Mercury and Venus are closer to the Sun than is the Earth. From our vantage point on Earth, there will be times when Mercury or Venus are between us and the Sun. Likewise, there will be times when the Sun is between us and Mercury or Venus. On the Zodiac wheel, the times when Mercury or Venus are at the same Zodiac sign and degree as the Earth are what astronomers call Conjunctions.

An Inferior Conjunction occurs with Mercury or Venus between Earth and the Sun. A Superior Conjunction occurs with the Sun between Earth and Mercury or Venus.

Conjunction events are closely related to Retrograde events in that they occur on either side of Retrograde events. For example, in 2015 Venus was Retrograde from late July to early September. Its actual Inferior Conjunction was recorded on August 15. Strangely enough, this Conjunction event aligned to a sharp market sell-off. When Venus emerges from Inferior Conjunction, it is visible as a Morning Star. When it emerges from Superior Conjunction it is visible as an Evening Star. Figure 10 illustrates the concept of Superior and Inferior Conjunction using Venus as an example.

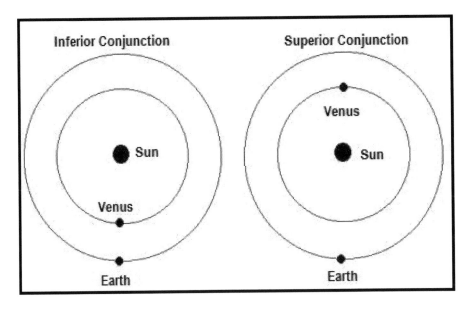

Figure 10 – Superior and Inferior Conjunction

Tools

Good data is the key to being able to apply Astrology to the financial markets.

To obtain a good part of this data, financial astrologers use Ephemeris Tables. For geocentric Astrology, the *New American Ephemeris for the 21st Century* is commonly used. It is available at most bookstores. For heliocentric Astrology, the *American Heliocentric Ephemeris* is a good resource. It tends to be harder to find in bookstores but on-line booksellers may have it available.

Data describing when planets are at maximum and minimum Elongation, Declination and at Superior and Inferior Conjunction tends to be a bit harder to find.

Thankfully, I have discovered the US Navy (in conjunction with the UK Hydrographic Office) publishes data tables each year. You can down load the 2016 tables at the website:

http://aa.usno.navy.mil/publications/reports/ap16_for_web.pdf

The 2017 data is at the following link:

http://aa.usno.navy.mil/publications/reports/ap17_for_web.pdf

For faster data access, an excellent software program is Solar Fire Gold produced by Astrolabe (www.alabe.com). I also use a market platform called Market Analyst. This brilliant piece of software, (originally developed in Australia) allows the user to generate an end of day price chart and then quickly overlay various astrological aspects and occurrences onto the chart. In my not so humble opinion, all serious adherents of Financial Astrology should spend the money to acquire this software program.

Quiz #1

Which planetary body corresponds to which of the following glyphs?
You will find the answer on the following page.

Here are the answers to Quiz #1. Keep practicing the task of memorizing these glyphs. Soon enough you will know them all too well which will make the application of Financial Astrology that much easier.

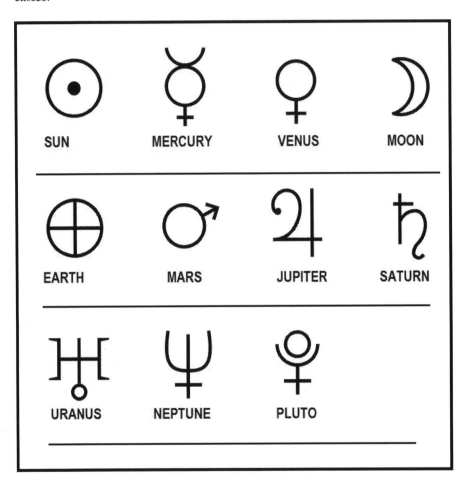

Quiz #2

Which Zodiac sign corresponds to which of the following glyphs ? You will find the answer on the following page.

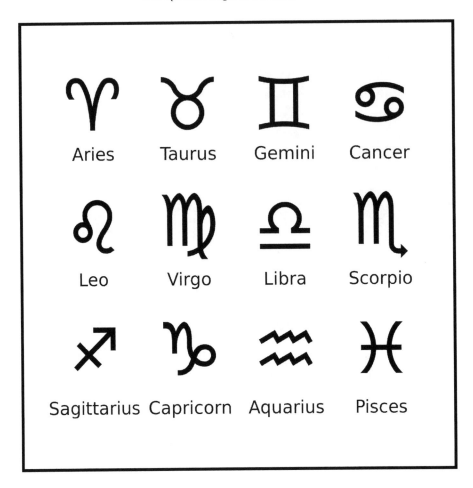

Aries	Taurus	Gemini	Cancer
Leo	Virgo	Libra	Scorpio
Sagittarius	Capricorn	Aquarius	Pisces

Here are the answers to Quiz #2. Keep practicing the task of memorizing these glyphs. Soon enough you will know them all too well. This knowledge combined with the knowledge of the planetary glyphs will make the application of Financial Astrology very enjoyable for you.

Quiz #3

Using your Ephemeris book or your software program, identify all the New Moon and Full Moon dates for calendar year 2017. You will find the answer on the following page. An alternative source is the downloadable PDF document from the US Navy found at:

http://aa.usno.navy.mil/publications/reports/ap17_for_web.pdf

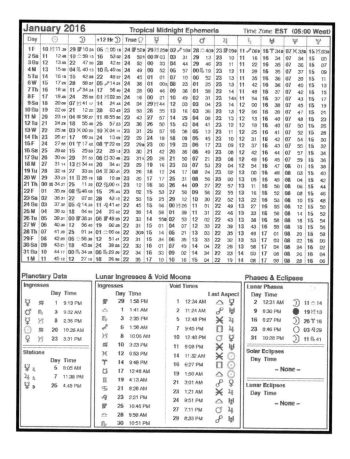

Full Moon		New Moon
		December 29, 2016
January 12		January 28
February 11		February 26
March 12		March 28
April 11		April 26
May 10		May 25
June 9		June 24
July 9		July 23
August 7		August 21
September 6		September 20
October 5		October 19
November 4		November 18
December 3		December 18

Here are the answers to Quiz #3. Keep practicing the task of using the Ephemeris Tables. Soon you will be able to navigate the data in the tables with great ease. Note that these answers are for the location Greenwich, England. If your Ephemeris table or software program is calibrated for another location, you may find your answers are off very slightly.

Quiz #4

Using your Ephemeris book or your software program, identify all the Mercury and Venus Retrograde events for 2017. You will find the answer on the following page.

Mercury		Venus
December 20, 2016 through to January 7, 2017		March 4 through April 14
April 9 through May 2		
August 13 through September 4		
December 3 through December 22		

Here are the answers to Quiz #4. Note also that if you were using an Ephemeris Table to ascertain these dates, typically Retrograde events are shaded a darker font in the Tables for easier identification.

Quiz #5

Using the data from the PDF version of the US Navy publication at:
http://aa.usno.navy.mil/publications/reports/ap17_for_web.pdf,
determine when Mercury will be at its maximum and minimum
Elongation points in 2017. Next, determine when Sun, Mars and Venus
will exhibit maximum and minimum Declination levels in 2017.

The answers are on the following page.

Sifting through the data table that starts on page 12 of the US Navy Report, you have found that Mercury will be at its greatest westerly Elongation on January 19, May 17 and September 12. Greatest easterly Elongation points are April 1, July 30 and November 24.

Using the Figure on page 8 of the US Navy document, Sun will be at its maximum declination in mid-June. This is what we call the Summer Solstice and the start of Summer. Sun will be at its minimum declination in mid-December. This is what we call the Winter Solstice and the start of Winter. Note also that Sun will be at 0 degrees of declination in mid-March and again in mid-September. These are the Equinoxes and mark the start of Spring and Autumn respectively.

Venus will reach an intermediate declination high in mid-March followed by a maximum in early August and a minimum in mid-December.

Mars will reach a Declination maximum in late May/early June.

What are your thoughts so far? If you are thinking that all this stuff is fairly straightforward, I am in agreement with you. I just wish that when I was learning this stuff I had had the benefit of a learning course such as this one.

From here on in, things get more interesting as I illustrate to you the practical part of applying Astrology to the markets.

3. The Trend

Read the financial section of your newspaper, read reports on-line or watch the business report on television and you are certain to hear lots of blather about quarterly earnings and corporate happenings. When was the last time you heard a business television media personality or a mainstream media journalist mention the trend? Probably never?

The trend is the best kept secret of the people who enjoy the most success with the markets. In 2002 as a rookie financial advisor I was fortunate to have had a veteran seasoned manager who drilled into my thick, stubborn head the notion of trend. I have never forgotten his sage advice and stern words. I have thanked him on many occasions, but somehow mere words do not seem to be adequate enough.

He enlightened me in two ways of measuring trend and both were developed nearly 40 years ago by legendary trader J. Wells Wilder. The first is the Wilder Volatility Stop and the second is the Directional Movement Indicator (DMI).

The mathematics behind each of these merits a book in itself. You do not have to understand the mathematics of each of these indicators, you just have to be able to apply these tools to a price chart. Most software programs that provide you with market quotes and charts will have these indicators built in. All you have to do is set the parameters.

If you do want to read Wilder's 1978 book, it is entitled *New Concepts in Technical Trading Systems* and in it you will learn the mathematical rigors behind these indicators.

For the Wilder Volatility Stop, I use a "study period" equal to 6. I then set the value for the constant "c" equal to somewhere in the range 2.0 to 2.8. What I am looking for is a value of "c" such that the indicator provides trend change signals in very close proximity to significant price highs and lows. Some software programs will have the value of "c" fixed at a whole integer. If that is the case, don't worry. You will find that a value of 2.0 probably works very well. For some stocks or commodities you may find that 3.0 is more appropriate.

For the Directional Movement Indicator, I use a study period of 14 on a daily chart and a study period of 9 on a weekly chart. All software programs that I have seen will allow you full control in setting this study period.

The best way to become conversant with the concept of trend is to study some examples.

Figure 11 presents a daily price chart of Facebook (Nasdaq:FB). I have overlaid the Wilder Volatility Stop with settings n=6 and c=2.0.

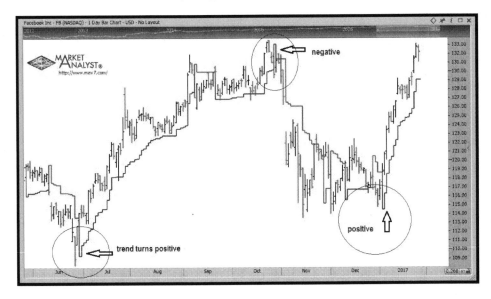

Figure 11 Facebook (FB) with Wilder Volatility

Note how the Wilder Volatility Stop closely aligns to significant price inflection points.

Figure 12 presents the same chart of Facebook with the 14 period Directional Movement Indicator overlaid in the lower panel of the chart. I have added dark vertical lines at the points where the DMI crosses over to a positive trend. As you can see, the DMI does a credible job of telling you when the trend has turned.

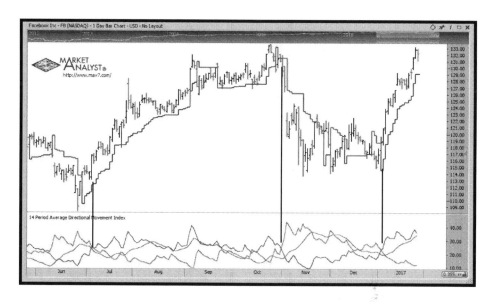

Figure 12 Facebook (FB) with DMI and Wilder

Figure 13 illustrates a daily price chart of Union Pacific Railway (NYSE: UNP). I have overlaid the Wilder Volatility Stop with n=6 and c=2.2. I have further overlaid the DMI with a 14 period setting.

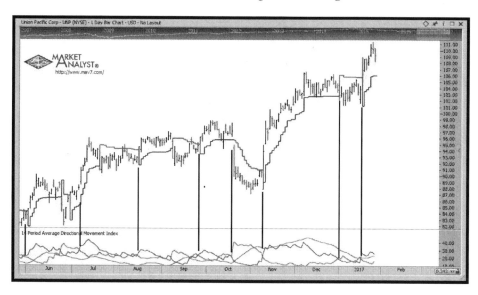

Figure 13 Union Pacific (UNP) with DMI and Wilder

This stock has had numerous short term trend changes, but these indicators seem to have captured them all.

These indicators extend into the realm of commodity futures trading as well.

Figure 14 illustrates a continuous front month daily price chart of Soybean futures. I have overlaid the Wilder Volatility Stop with n=6 and c=2.2. I have further overlaid the DMI with a 14 period setting. As you can see, commodity futures by their very speculative nature tend to be quite volatile, with trend sometimes swinging back and forth between favorable and unfavorable very quickly. However, the Wilder Volatility Stop and the DMI do a credible job of catching most of the trend swings. With commodity futures, you may also wish to employ shorter timeframe charts and other tools such as moving averages. If you are a skilled trader, you will know what to do. If you are not skilled at trading commodity futures, I suggest sticking to stocks.

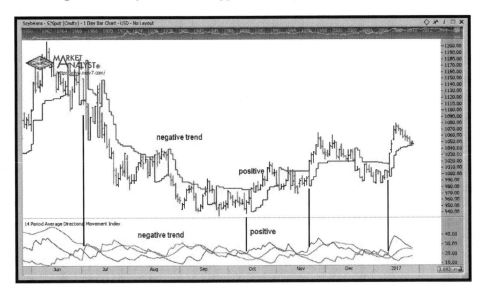

Figure 14 Soybeans with DMI and Wilder

I will wrap up this brief chapter with a look at the British Pound. Figure 15 illustrates the continuous front month daily price chart of the

Pound. I have overlaid the Wilder Volatility Stop with n=6 and c=3.0. I have further overlaid the DMI with a 14 period setting.

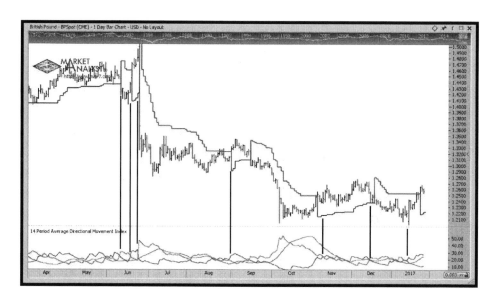

Figure 15 British Pound with DMI and Wilder

Carefully watching the Wilder Stop or the DMI would have warned you that something was amiss in June 2016 when in a short span of time the trend moved from positive to negative to positive and finally back to negative. What was amiss was that the forces in favor of Brexit were gaining momentum. And in June, the citizens voted to leave the European Union, much to the shock of the media and world leaders.

The purpose of this short chapter was to illustrate that trend can indeed be measured. With Financial Astrology, one will be watching for the trend to change as an astrological event arrives. Not every event is strong enough to alter the trend. But most are. You do not necessarily have to trade at each event by getting in or out of the market. You may simply wish to place a protective stop loss order such that if the trend changes in a severe way, you do not incur severe losses on your position. In the remainder of this learning Course I will show numerous examples of how various astrological events have influenced stocks, commodity futures and market indices. After you have thoroughly studied these examples, you will be able to generate charts of stocks that you like and overlay astrological events using data from an Ephemeris, the US Navy data tables or a software program.

Practical Exercise

As a practical exercise, I now encourage you to generate some stock or commodity charts and practice overlaying them with the Wilder Volatility Stop and the DMI. Get comfortable recognizing trend changes.

4. Financial Astrology in Action

Mercury Retrograde

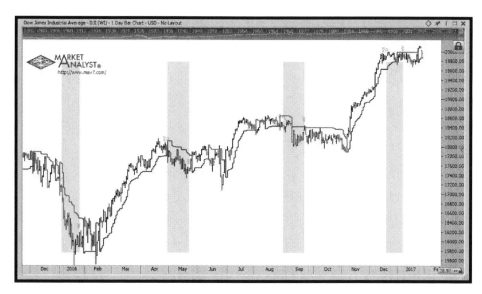

Figure 16 – Mercury Retrograde and the Dow Jones Average

Earlier in this Course, I explained the notion of Retrograde. I asked you to use the data tables to determine Retrograde events for 2017. Now, let's take a look at how you can use Mercury Retrograde in your trading and investing.

To illustrate the use of Mercury Retrograde, consider the Dow Jones Average chart in Figure 16 above. The timeframe in this chart is from 2016. Mercury Retrograde events are illustrated by the dark shared bars overlaid on the chart. Notice how all too often these bars align to sharp swings in trend.

In late 2015, markets started to weaken and the trend turned negative. But, January 2016 brought a Mercury Retrograde event and the trend turned positive again. May 2016 saw a brief spell of negative trend. September 2016 saw the onset of a negative trend again, but this time the damage was not severe. December 2016 saw another Retrograde event and the trend actually turned negative when the Dow struggled on several occasions to surpass the 20,000 mark.

Venus Retrograde

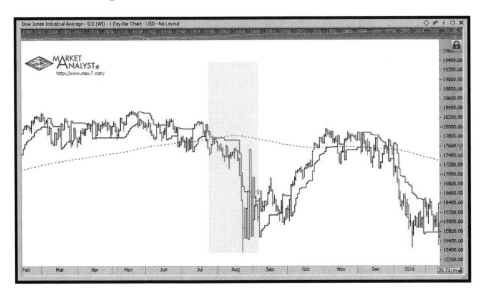

Figure 17 – Venus Retrograde and the Dow Jones Average

To illustrate the use of Venus Retrograde as a tool to assist one with trading or investing, consider the chart in Figure 17 above. The timeframe in this chart is from 2015 as Venus exhibits far fewer Retrograde events than Mercury. The Venus Retrograde event is illustrated by the dark shared bar overlaid on the chart. In this particular case, in June-July, the Dow flirted dangerously with its 200 day moving average – shown as a dashed line. When the Dow finally did break the 200 day average, investors were wondering just what was happening. Venus Retrograde was happening –that's what. Note the damage done to the Dow during this powerful event. No sooner did Venus wrap up its Retrograde event than the trend resumed its upward journey.

Imagine if you had been able to take advantage of this event because you had the power of Financial Astrology working for you. Imagine also playing the market three or four times a year at Mercury Retrograde events. If all you ever did was use Astrology to pursue

Retrograde events, you will probably come out ahead of a good many other traders and investors.

Mars Retrograde

Mars Retrograde does not affect all markets in a like manner. One market where Mars Retrograde events tend to deliver sharp volatility is the 10 Year Treasury Note Futures.

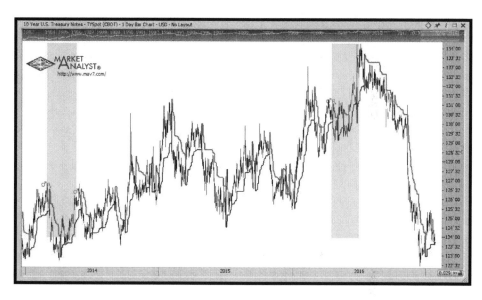

Figure 18 – Mars Retrograde and the 10 Year Treasury Note Futures

The 10 Year Treasuries are volatile enough to begin with. However, traders of these futures should be alert for sharp price swings and trend changes during Mars Retrograde events as Figure 18 illustrates. In this chart, a Mars retrograde event in 2014 aligned to a short term trend change but also to a significant low. In 2016, interest rates (yield on the 10 year Treasuries) hit their lows just as Mars completed a Retrograde event.

Check back across earlier time frames for stocks that you follow to see if there is a correlation to Mars Retrograde events. Remember, not all stocks will exhibit a correlation to Mars Retrograde. To illustrate, consider the price chart of Goldman Sachs (NYSE:GS) shown in Figure 19. This is one stock that I have found that does align to Mars Retrograde. In 2014 and again in 2016, Mars Retrograde events made for enticing entry points.

Figure 19 – Mars Retrograde and Goldman Sachs (GS)

Venus and Mars Declination

In 1946, noted astrologer Donald Bradley (a.k.a. Garth Allen) developed what has come to be called the Bradley Model or the Bradley Siderograph. Its intent was to provide a model for predicting price action on the Dow Jones Average. The mathematical equation for this gnarly beast of a model is a tough one involving sinusoidal mathematics. But, two variables stand out in the model – the Declination of Venus and the declination of Mars.

To this day, I find it intriguing that markets have a high propensity to deliver a trend change at maximum and/or minimum Declination points of Venus and Mars. Recall that Declination refers to the movement of planets above and below the equatorial ecliptic as viewed from our vantage point here on Earth. If you are using an Astrology software program, it will likely generate Declination plots for you that resemble what you saw in Figure 8. If you do not have software, the image on page 8 of the US Navy data publication provides a basic plot.

To illustrate the use of Declination as a tool to help one navigate the financial markets consider the following chart in Figure 20 where Venus Declination events have been overlaid onto a chart of the STOXX 50 Index from 2012 to mid-2015. As noted earlier, the Market Analyst software program is pricy, but its ease of use in overlaying astrological phenomena onto charts is well worth the price. Note the short term trend shifts as Venus approaches, records and then leaves its maximum Declination. Similarly, note the like behavior at the minimum Declination points.

I do not recommend using Declination as a pinpoint precision instrument. Rather, as a Declination maximum or minimum event is unfolding over a period of days, use either the DMI or Wilder trend indicators to alert you to trend shifts.

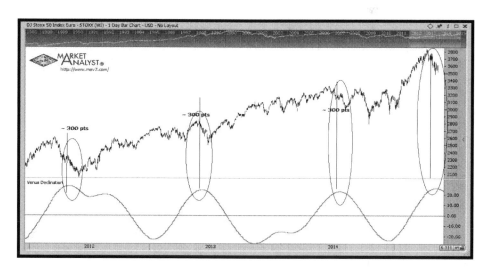

Figure 20 Venus Declination and Stoxx 50

As a further example, consider the chart of the Dow Jones in Figure 21. Note how Mars Declination maxima and minima align to trend changes.

So, no need to really master the detailed construct of the Bradley Model. Just keep your eye fixed on the Declination patterns of Venus and Mars.

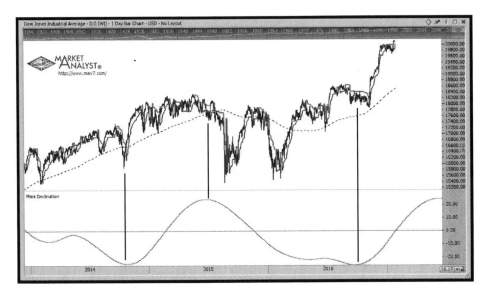

Figure 21 Mars Declination and the Dow Jones

Not every individual stock's price action will adhere to these Declination points. Check some of your favorite stocks and see if there is a correlation. To show an example of a stock that has reasonable correlation, consider the chart of Conoco Phillips (NYSE:COP) in Figure 22.

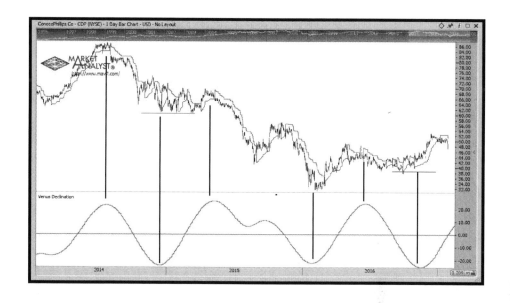

Figure 22 Conoco Phillips and Venus Declination

Note how in 2014, a maximum in Venus Declination aligned to a peak in the stock price and a serious trend change. In late 2014, some price stability was found at Venus minimum Declination. In 2015 another price decline set in at a Declination maxima. Early 2016 saw a share price low at a Declination minima. Mid-2016 saw share price encounter stiff resistance and lapse into a sideways trend at a maxima point of Declination. An uptrend again resumed in late 2016 at a Declination minima.

Mercury Elongation

As discussed earlier, Elongation refers to the apparent angle that an orbiting planet makes with the Sun as viewed from our vantage point here on Earth. The planet Mercury tends to be the planet most used in Elongation studies. To illustrate the effects of Mercury Elongation, consider the chart in Figure 23 from the 2015 timeframe.

During 2015, Mercury was at its maximum easterly Elongation on January 14, May 7, September 4 and December 29. During 2015,

Mercury was at its maximum westerly Elongation on February 24, June 24 and October 16.

These points of maximum easterly and westerly Elongation are marked on the chart as "E" and "W".

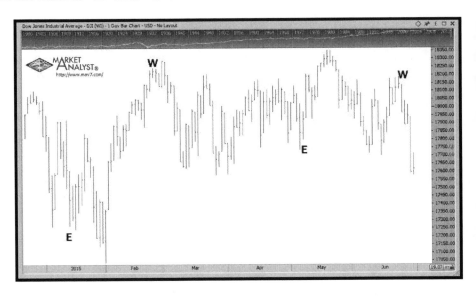

Figure 23 Mercury Elongation and the Dow Jones Average

To illustrate further, consider the chart in Figure 24 which illustrates price action of the Australian Stock Market and the ASX 200 Index.

Figure 24 ASX 200 and Mercury Elongation

The timeframe in the above chart of the ASX 200 is from late 2015 through to early 2017.

For 2016, Mercury was at its maximum easterly Elongation on April 18, August 16 and again on December 11. Mercury was at its maximum westerly Elongations on February 7, June 5 and September 28.

In late 2015, Mercury at its greatest easterly Elongation aligned with a significant change in trend to the downside. The trend then changed for the better at a point of maximum westerly Elongation. A point of easterly Elongation in April 2016 aligned to a nasty dip and a pause to the uptrend. A peak and a trend change came at westerly Elongation in June. And so it goes. Note at the far right of the chart, the Inauguration of President Donald J. Trump took place merely 1 day after a point of Mercury maximum westerly Elongation. The world has been on edge ever since waiting for the latest Twitter feed and Executive Order.

Imagine now being able to be on alert as Mercury is making its points of greatest east and west Elongation. Imagine being able to take action to protect your investments at these critical times as others that you know get thrashed around in the markets.

Superior and Inferior Conjunctions

Earlier, I introduced you to the notion of Superior and Inferior Conjunction. I pointed out that Venus and Mercury were the two planets of most interest when studying Conjunction. During 2015, Mercury was at Inferior Conjunction on January 30, May 30 and September 23. During 2015, Mercury was at Superior Conjunction at April 10, July 23 and November 17.

The chart of the Dow Jones average in Figure 25 has been overlaid with Mercury Inferior (triangle shape) and Superior (circle) Conjunctions.

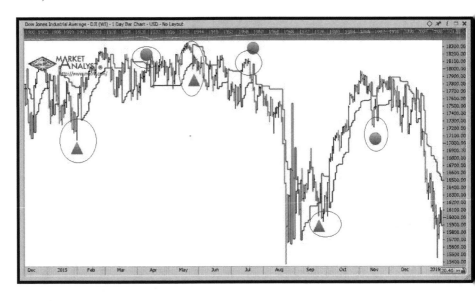

Figure 25 Dow and Mercury Conjunctions

Remember – the Mercury Inferior Conjunction events will always occur during a Mercury Retrograde event. While the Inferior Conjunction event itself may not always align to a short term trend change, the overall Retrograde event most likely will.

In recent years, Venus has exhibited Inferior Conjunctions on June 6, 2012, January 11, 2014 and August 15, 2015. March 25, 2017 will see Venus at Inferior Conjunction again. Superior Conjunctions have occurred recently at March 28, 2013, October 25, 2014 and June 6, 2016. The next Superior Conjunction will be at January 9, 2018.

Whenever Venus records a Superior Conjunction event, it will shortly thereafter appear to the observer as an Evening Star. After recording an Inferior Conjunction, it will appear as a Morning Star.

The following chart of the Dow Jones illustrates these Inferior (star shape) and Superior Conjunction (diamond shape) events.

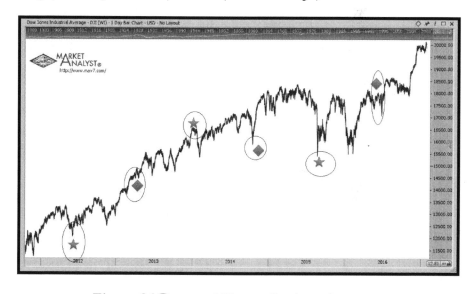

Figure 26 Dow and Venus Conjunctions

This chart covers a wide span of time. It helps to take a closer look at one of these Venus events. Consider the chart in Figure 27 which better illustrates the June 6, 2016 Superior Conjunction.

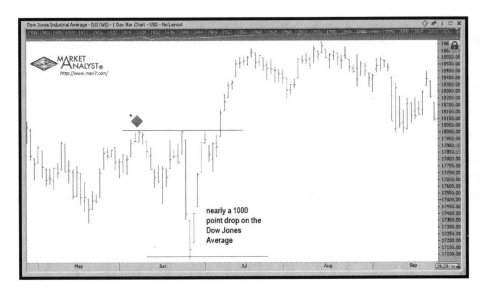

Figure 27 Dow and Venus Superior Conjunction of June 2016

Note that this event created nearly a 1000 point drop in the Dow Jones. Imagine now, if you had knowledge of financial astrology and were closely watching the trend. You could have easily sidestepped much of this market carnage.

Other Markets

Let's now take a look at some other markets. I think you will agree that Astrology is widespread.

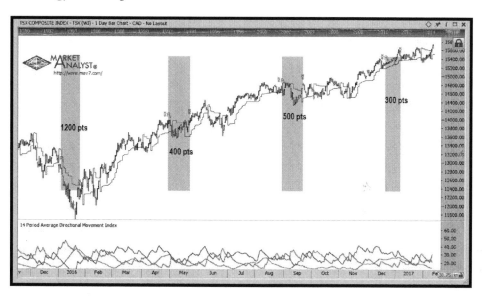

Figure 28 Toronto Exchange and Mercury Retrograde

Figure 28 shows that Mercury Retrograde events can impact the Toronto Stock Exchange. The effect may not be as pronounced as on the Dow Jones, but there will be an impact.

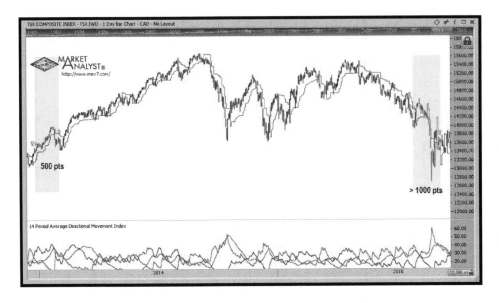

Figure 29 Toronto Exchange and Venus Retrograde

Figure 29 shows that the Toronto Stock Exchange is also impacted by Venus Retrograde events. The 2015 event at the right part of the chart shows that the trend had already turned negative. As Venus Retrograde set in, the trend briefly tried to turn positive, but failed and the negative trend then re-asserted itself with a vengeance.

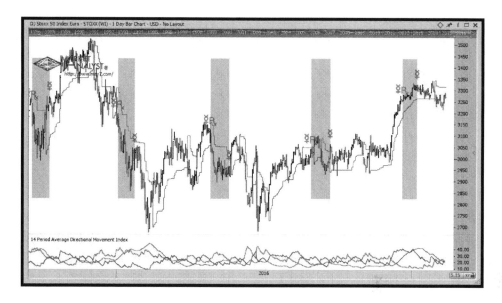

Figure 30 Stoxx 50 Index and Mercury Retrograde

Figure 30 illustrates that Mercury Retrograde events in fact do impact the Stoxx 50 Index. Note that the event in early 2016 saw an acceleration of the downtrend, as the trend had already gone negative in late 2015.

Figure 31 Stoxx 50 Index and Venus Retrograde

Figure 31 illustrates that the Stoxx 50 Index is affected by Venus Retrograde. What is interesting is the magnitude of the impact – small in 2014 and larger in 2015.

Figure 32 Australia XJO and Mercury Conjunctions

Figure 32 illustrates that in Australia the XJO (ASX 200) is impacted by Mercury Conjunctions. Both Inferior and Superior events have been overlaid on the chart above. Impacts are variable in size, but bear watching nonetheless. Remember that the 0 degree Conjunctions also are Retrograde events. For example, at the right of the chart, it appears like the Mercury Conjunction had no bearing at all. As a practical exercise, check to see when Mercury was Retrograde in late 2016. Now look at the correlation to the market peak.

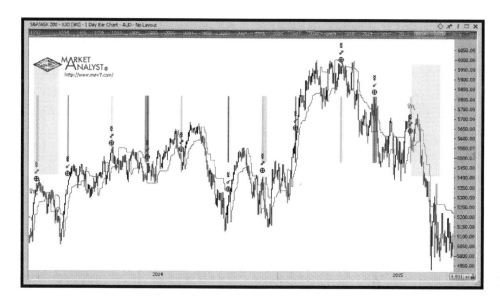

Figure 33 Australia XJO and Venus Retrograde

Figure 33 illustrates that Venus Retrograde events also impact the XJO (ASX 200). The magnitude of the impact will vary, but taking advantage of these events can add to your trading and investing success.

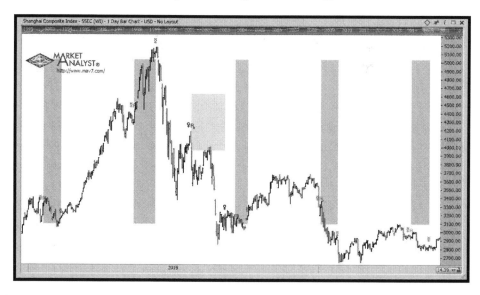

Figure 34 Shanghai and Retrograde Events

Figure 34 illustrates that Mercury and Venus Retrograde events even have a bearing on the Shanghai market. The Venus event is depicted by the smaller rectangle in the middle part of the above chart.

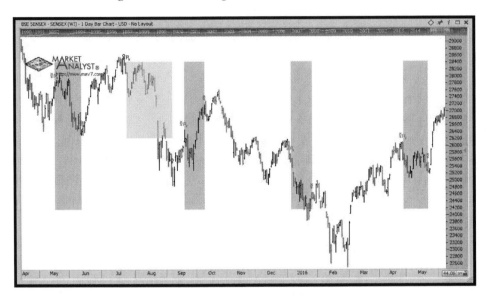

Figure 35 Bombay SENSEX and Retrograde Events

I routinely get email inquiries from people in India asking if I know anything about Vedic Astrology in the context of the Indian stock market. Of course, I know nothing about anything Vedic. But, judging from the chart in Figure 53, maybe a person in India should just focus on western Astrology as it appears that Mercury and Venus Retrograde events do impact the Bombay market. I am sure that other astro events will have an impact too. In Figure 35, the Venus event is the smaller rectangle towards the left part of the chart.

And let's look at a couple final charts. First – the German DAX. Figure 36 shows that the DAX is impacted by Venus Declination.

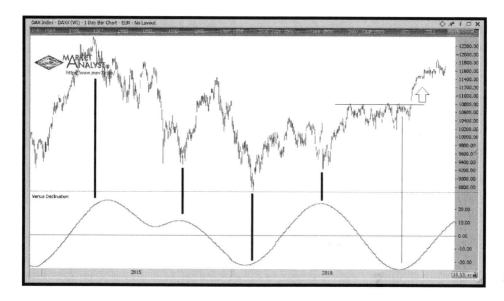

Figure 36 DAX and Venus Declination

In Figure 36, I have inserted heavier darker lines to show the connection between Declination maxima and minima to price inflection points. The event at the right side of the chart is intriguing. The market was trending sideways with little conviction and once the Declination low was recorded, the market surged higher.

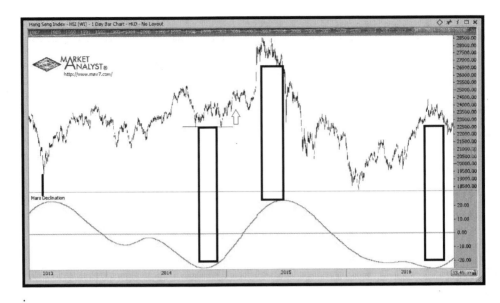

Figure 37 Hang Seng and Mars Declination

And finally, the Hang Seng in Hong Kong. I am getting more and more newsletter subscribers from China who are managing to find me on-line. Judging from Figure 34 previous and Figure 37 following, there appears to be a correlation to Astrology on the Hong Kong market as well as Shanghai.

5. Encouraging Final Words

If you have made it this far, I commend you for your open mind. Most people cannot make it this far because they think in such a linear fashion. Their belief-set paradigms also mentally prevent them from embracing something as esoteric as Astrology.

I have introduced you to the fundamentals of Astrology and shown you the very basics of Financial Astrology. I have quizzed you to show that none of this stuff is really all that hard. With access to the data, you can quickly make some valuable determinations. I have hopefully impressed upon you the connection between the price trend and astrological events. And I hope I have given you enough examples to whet your appetite and launch you on a journey that I am sure will change the way you view the financial markets.

If this is the only of the Principia Astrologia learning Courses you decide to undertake, then you have enough ammunition at your disposal right here, right now to seriously alter your trading and investing experiences.

If you are yearning for more, then I invite you to acquire the two other Courses which will propel you to even greater heights.

As you embrace Financial Astrology as a valuable tool to assist you in your trading and investing activity, I further hope also that you will pause often to reflect on the deeper connection between the financial markets, Astrology and the emotions of mankind.

On that note, I will leave you with the words of Neil Turok from his 2012 book, *The Universe Within*.

"Perseverance leads to enlightenment. And the truth is more beautiful than your wildest dreams".

6. Glossary of Terms

Ascendant: One of four cardinal points on a horoscope, the Ascendant is situated in the East.

Aspect: The angular relationship between two planets measured in degrees.

Autumnal Equinox: (see Equinox) – That time of year when Sun is at 0 degrees Libra.

Conjunct: An angular relationship of 0 degrees between two planets.

Cosmo-biology: Changes in human emotion caused by changes in cosmic energy.

Descendant: One of four cardinal points on a horoscope, the Descendant is situated in the West.

Ephemeris: A daily tabular compilation of planetary and lunar positions.

Equinox: An event occurring twice annually, an equinox event marks the time when the tilt of the Earth's axis is neither toward or away from the Sun.

First Trade chart: A zodiac chart depicting the positions of the planets at the time a company's stock or a commodity future commenced trading on a recognized financial exchange.

First Trade date: The date a stock or commodity futures contract first began trading on a recognized exchange.

Full Moon: From a vantage point situated on Earth, when the Moon is seen to be 180 degrees to the Sun.

Geocentric Astrology: That version of Astrology in which the vantage point for determining planetary aspects is the Earth.

Heliocentric Astrology: That version of Astrology in which the vantage point for determining planetary aspects is the Sun.

House: A 1/12th portion of the zodiac. Portions are not necessarily equal depending on the mathematical formula used to calculate the divisions.

Lunar Eclipse: A lunar eclipse occurs when the Sun, Earth, and Moon are aligned exactly, or very closely so, with the Earth in the middle. The Earth blocks the Sun's rays from striking the Moon.

Lunar Month: (see Synodic Month.

Lunation: (see New Moon.)

Mid-Heaven: One of four cardinal points on a horoscope, the Mid-Heaven is situated in the South.

New Moon: From a vantage point situated on Earth, when the Moon is seen to be 0 degrees to the Sun.

North Node of Moon: The intersection points between the Moon's plane and Earth's ecliptic are termed the North and South nodes. Astrologers tend to focus on the North node and Ephemeris tables clearly list the zodiacal position of the North Node for each calendar day.

Orb: The amount of flexibility or tolerance given to an aspect.

Retrograde motion: The apparent backwards motion of a planet through the zodiac signs when viewed from a vantage point on Earth.

Sidereal Month: The Moon orbits Earth with a slightly elliptical pattern in approximately 27.3 days, relative to a fixed frame of reference.

Sidereal Orbital Period: The time required for a planet to make one full orbit of the Sun as viewed from a fixed vantage point on the Sun.

Siderograph: A mathematical equation developed by astrologer Donald Bradley in 1946 (By plotting the output of the equation against date, inflection points can be seen on the plotted curve. It is at these inflection points that human emotion is most apt to change resulting in a trend change on the Dow Jones or S&P 500 Index).

Solar Eclipse: A solar eclipse occurs when the Moon passes between the Sun and Earth and fully or partially blocks the Sun.

Solstice: Occurring twice annually, a solstice event marks the time when the Sun reaches its highest or lowest altitude above the horizon at noon.

Synodic Month: During a sidereal month (see Sidereal Month), Earth will revolve part way around the Sun thus making the average apparent time between one New Moon and the next New Moon longer than the sidereal month at approximately 29.5 days. This 29.5 day time span is called a Synodic Month or sometimes a Lunar Month.

Synodic Orbital Period: The time required for a planet to make one full orbit of the Sun as viewed from a fixed vantage point on Earth.

Vernal Equinox: That time of the year when Sun is at 0 degrees Aries.

Zodiac: An imaginary band encircling the 360 degrees of the planetary system divided into twelve equal portions of 30 degrees each.

Zodiac Wheel: A circular image broken into 12 portions of 30 degrees each. Each portion represents a different astrological sign.

7. Other Books By the Author

Once maligned by many, the subject of financial Astrology is now experiencing a revival as traders and investors seek deeper insight into the forces that move the financial markets.

The markets are a dynamic entity fueled by many factors, some of which we can easily comprehend, some of which are esoteric. This book introduces the reader to the notion that astrological phenomena can influence price action on financial markets and create trend changes across both short and longer term time horizons. From an introduction to the historical basics behind Astrology through to an examination of lunar Astrology and planetary aspects, the numerous illustrated examples in this book will introduce the reader the power of Astrology and its impact on both equity markets and commodity futures markets.

The financial markets are a reflection of the psychological emotions of traders and investors. These emotions ebb and flow in harmony with the forces of nature.

Scientific techniques and phenomena such as square root mathematics, the Golden Mean, the Golden Sequence, lunar events, planetary transits and planetary aspects have been used by civilizations dating as far back as the ancient Egyptians in order to comprehend the forces of nature.

The emotions of traders and investors can be seen to fluctuate in accordance with these forces of nature. Lunar events can be seen to align with trend changes on financial markets. Significant market cycles can be seen to align with planetary transits and aspects. Price patterns on stocks, commodity futures and market indices can be seen to conform to square root and Golden Mean mathematics.

In the early years of the 20th century the most successful traders on Wall Street, including the venerable W.D. Gann, used these scientific techniques and phenomena to profit from the markets. However, over the ensuing decades as technology has advanced, the science has been lost.

The Lost Science acquaints the reader with an extensive range of astrological and mathematical phenomena. From the Golden Mean and Fibonacci Sequence, to planetary transit lines and square roots through to an examination of lunar Astrology and planetary aspects, the numerous illustrated examples in this book will show the reader how these unique scientific phenomena impact the financial markets.

Very little is known about Louise McWhirter, except that in 1937 she wrote the book *McWhirter Theory of Stock Market Forecasting.*

In my travels to places as far away as the British Library in London, England to research financial Astrology, not once did I come across any other books by her. Not once did I find any other book from her era that even mentioned her name. All of this I find to be deeply mysterious. Whoever she was – she wrote only one book, and it was a powerful one that is as accurate today as it was back in 1937. The purpose of writing this book is suggested by the title itself – to de-mystify McWhirter's methodology - which is not exactly straightforward.

Can the movements of the Moon affect the stock market?

Are price swings on Crude Oil, Soybeans, the British pound and other financial instruments a reflection of planetary placements?

The answer to these questions is YES. Changes in price trends on the markets are in fact related to our changing emotions. Our emotions in turn are impacted by the changing events in our cosmos.

In the early part of the 20th century many successful traders on Wall Street, including the venerable W.D. Gann and the mysterious Louise McWhirter, understood that emotion was linked to the forces of the cosmos. They used astrological events and esoteric mathematics to predict changes in price trend and to profit from the markets.

However, in the latter part of the 20th century, the investment community has become more comfortable just relying on academic financial theory and the opinions of colorful television media personalities all wrapped up in a buy and hold mentality.

The Cosmic Clock has been written for traders and investors who are seeking to gain an understanding of the cosmic forces that influence emotion and the financial markets.

8. About The Author

Malcolm Bucholtz, B.Sc, MBA is a graduate of Queen's University Faculty of Engineering in Canada and Heriot Watt University in Scotland where he received an MBA degree. After working in Canadian industry for far too many years, Malcolm followed his passion for the financial markets by becoming an Investment Advisor/Commodity Trading Advisor with an independent brokerage firm in western Canada. Today, he resides in western Canada where he trades the financial markets using technical chart analysis, esoteric mathematics and the astrological principles outlined in this book.

Malcolm is the author of several books. His first book, *The Bull, the Bear and the Planets*, offers the reader an introduction to Financial Astrology and makes the case that there are esoteric and astrological phenomena that influence the financial markets. His second book, *The Lost Science*, takes the reader on a deeper journey into planetary events and unique mathematical phenomena that influence financial markets. His third book, *De-Mystifying the McWhirter Theory of Stock Market Forecasting* seeks to simplify and illustrate the McWhirter methodology. The Cosmic Clock is designed for people seeking to gain insight into the forces that influence the financial markets.

In addition, each year Malcolm releases a Financial Astrology Almanac. The 2017 Financial Astrology Almanac shows the reader the critical dates to watch for in 2017.

Malcolm maintains both a website (www.investingsuccess.ca) and a blog where he provides traders and investors with astrological insights into the financial markets. He also offers a bi-weekly **Astrology E-Alert** service where subscribers receive previews of pending astrological events that stand to influence markets.

37611579R00049

Made in the USA
Middletown, DE
28 February 2019